T0020988

Wait a second! Did an elephant plant a tree?

They went on a field trip and planted trees! What fun!

A teacher taught her students all about trees.

Oops! The tasty berry fell. The wren planted a juniper tree!

A wren flies to her nest with a juniper berry in her beak.

It wasn't long before a seed grew into a date palm tree!

A camel chewed some dates and then spit the seeds out.

It pooped seeds. Trees were planted all over the rainforest!

In the Amazon River, a pacu ate floating fruit.

Later, the owl coughed up an owl pellet and an elm tree grew!

An owl swallowed a mouse that had been eating elm tree seeds.

It walked and walked. As pears fell off, trees were planted!

A moose got a pear tree branch stuck in its antlers.

They planted fig trees! Stop it! Don't throw food!

Playful monkeys threw figs at each other.

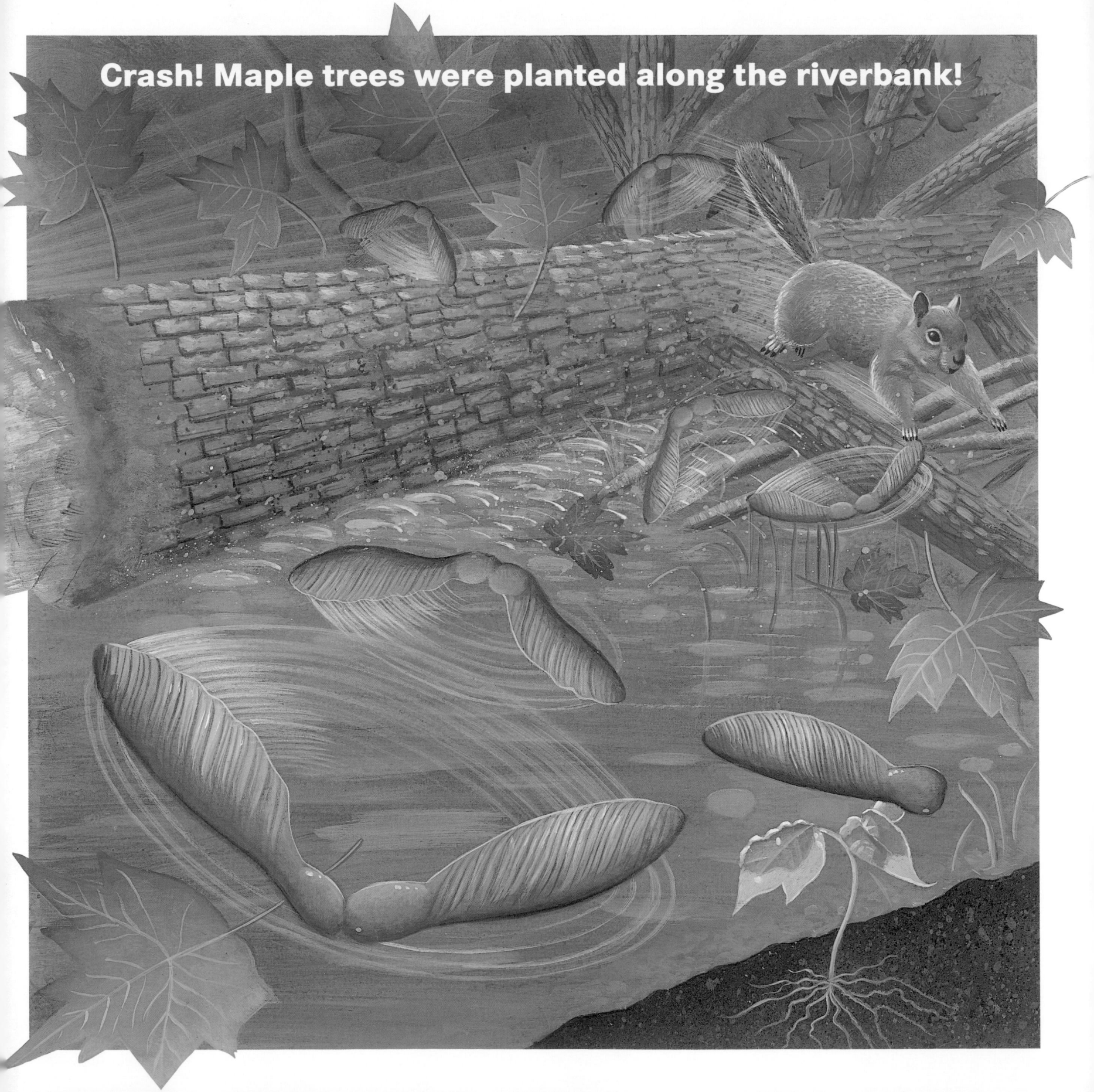
Crash! Maple trees were planted along the riverbank!

A beaver used his sharp teeth to chop down a maple tree.

She swished her tail. A seed fell and grew into a cherry tree!

Cherry seeds got caught on the tail of a wild horse.

They didn’t know it. They planted a pine tree!

Ants marched a pine nut down their tunnel.

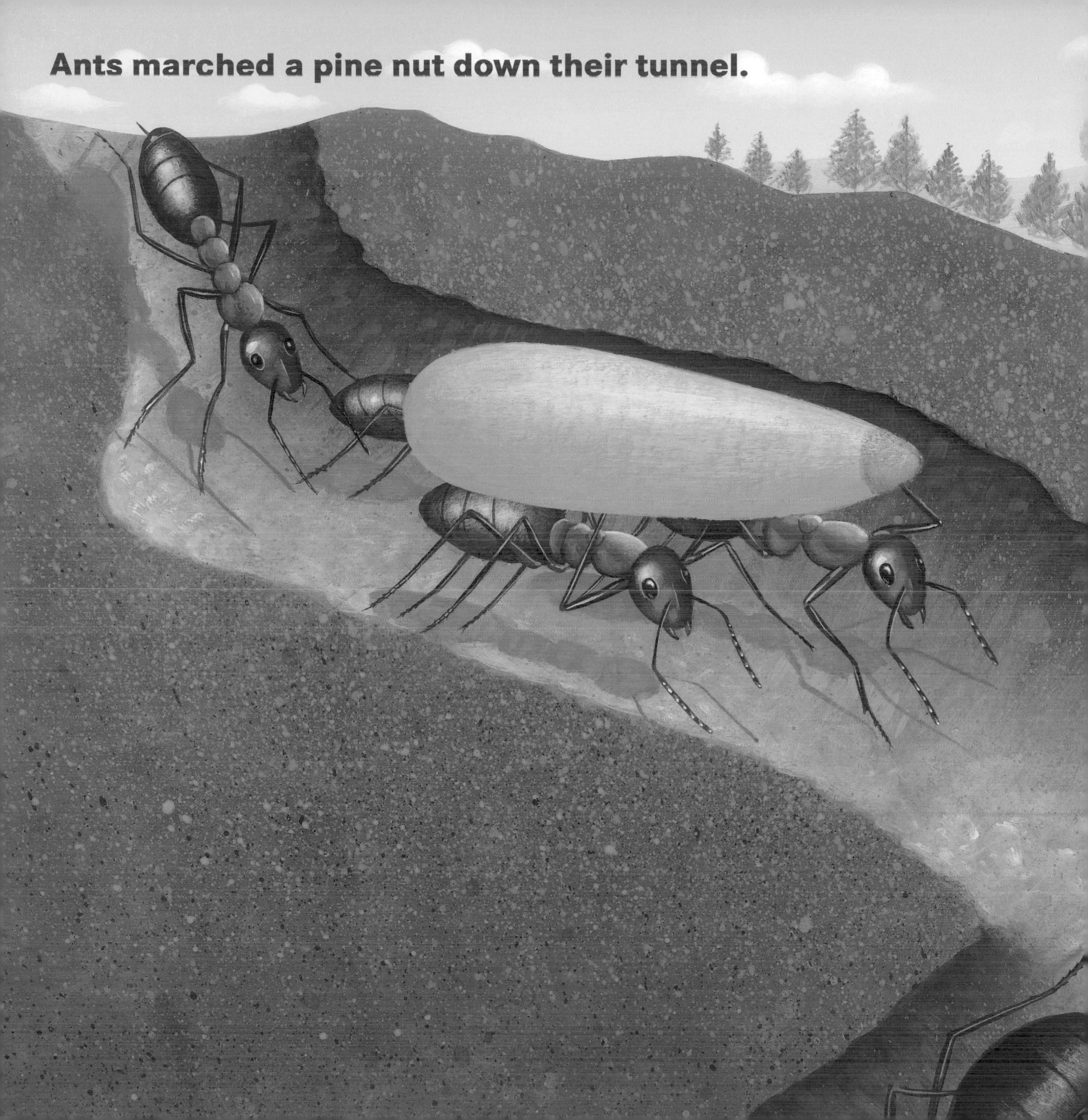

The coconut floated to an island and a palm tree grew!

A dolphin pushed a coconut into ocean currents.

Miles away, the burr came off. She planted a chestnut tree!

A goose migrated with a chestnut burr stuck to her feathers.

The bear tripped, a seed fell off, and he planted an apple tree!

Seeds stuck to the messy fur of an apple-eating black bear.

He didn’t know it, but he planted an oak tree!

Last fall a squirrel buried an acorn.

I wonder who will plant a tree?

To Abby, Hannah, and Emma, who planted a tree of joy in my head

J. P.

For my agent, Libby Ford

T. L.

Text Copyright © 2010 Jerry Pallotta
Illustration Copyright © 2010 Tom Leonard

All rights reserved. No part of this book may be reproduced in any manner without the express written consent of the publisher, except in the case of brief excerpts in critical reviews and articles. All inquiries should be addressed to:

Sleeping Bear Press
2395 S. Huron Parkway, Suite 200
Ann Arbor MI 48104
www.sleepingbearpress.com

Printed and bound in the United States.

15 16 17 18 19 20

Library of Congress Cataloging-in-Publication Data

Pallotta, Jerry.
Who will plant a tree? / written by Jerry Pallotta ; illustrated by Tom Leonard.
p. cm
ISBN 978-1-58536-502-9
1. Trees–Seeds–Dispersal–Juvenile literature. 2. Seeds–Dispersal–Juvenile literature.
I. Leonard, Thomas, 1955- II. Title.
QK929.P35 2010
582.16–dc22 2009037411

Who Will Plant a Tree?

Written by Jerry Pallotta and Illustrated by Tom Leonard

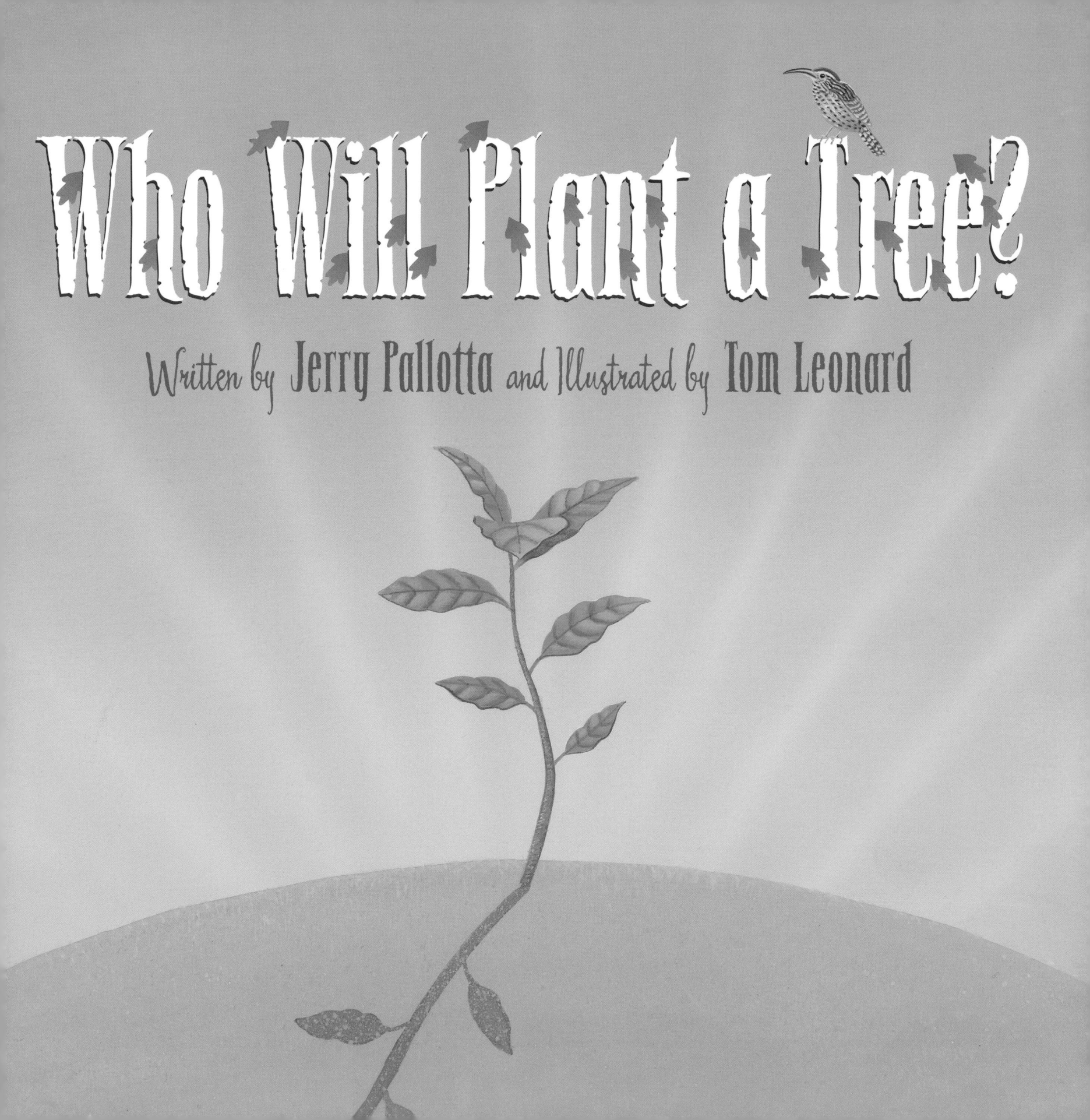